The Book of
Ashoka
Warrior Prince
to
Emperor of Peace

Also from the Langley Press

An African Testament:
Solomon and the Queen of Sheba

The Life and Legend of Nicholas Flamel,
Discoverer of the Philosopher's Stone

Mary Ann Cotton: Victorian Serial Killer

Thomas Bewick: Great Northern Artist

In Search of the Celtic Saints

In Search of the Little Count

The Lambton Worm

For free downloads and more from the Langley Press,
please visit our website at:

http://tinyurl.com/lpdirect

The Book of
Ashoka

Cover photo of Ashoka lion capital at Sanchi in Madhya Pradesh, India by Yann Forget

To my friend,
Joan Cuthbertson

Contents

Jawaharlal Nehru

Introduction

Before he became the first prime minister of India in 1947, Jawaharlal Nehru spent some nine years in various prisons under the British. From prison he would write to his daughter Indira who, as Indira Gandhi, would later become the third prime minister of India in her own right. Some of Nehru's letters to his daughter included his own 'take' on Indian history; and he re-told for her the remarkable life-story of Ashoka Maurya, the compassionate, enlightened emperor of a vast Indian empire in the third century BCE.

As a left-leaning republican who looked forward to the disappearance of all monarchies, Indira's father was slightly embarrassed to be praising a man who had inherited his grandfather's empire through his father. He quoted the treatment of Ashoka by H.G. Wells, an English writer of an earlier generation whose thoughts on the celebrated emperor are reprinted below.

As another left-leaning thinker, Wells must also have felt rather awkward about singling out one of the tribe he calls 'their majesties and graciousnesses and serenities and royal highnesses and the like' for praise; but in his letters about Ashoka, Nehru implies that Indians cannot but look back on Ashoka's regime with pride. In fact, Ashoka's example of virtuous rule remains an inspiration for Indians today. A lion-headed capital fashioned for the Maurya emperor is still an official symbol of India, and the wheel at the centre of the

Indian flag is the Ashokachakra.

Ashoka makes a good role-model for modern Indians partly because, as a Buddhist, he was not a Hindu, Christian or Muslim, so it is more difficult for him to become a divisive figure (as we shall see, there are very few Indian Buddhists today). Ashoka could not have become either a Christian or a Muslim in any case, because the founders of both Christianity and Islam were born centuries after he died. His status as a role-model for modern Indians is also a reminder that though the majority of Indians are now either Hindus or Muslims, Buddhism was once dominant in many parts of India, and in other places that are now predominantly Muslim. The fact that Ashoka was responsible for a major expansion of the Buddhist religion has tempted western historians to compare him to Constantine the Great, the Roman emperor who promoted Christianity throughout his own empire.

Although Ashoka is now a patriotic Indian hero, the full extent of his remarkable achievement as a leader had been forgotten by Indians until it was revealed by European researchers. By 1838, the year of Queen Victoria's coronation, a brilliant young Englishman called James Princep had worked out how to read the Brahmi alphabet in which a number of mysterious Indian inscriptions had been cut in stone. Little-known today, Princep's name should be spoken in the same breath as the names of those other great European code-breakers; Alan Turing, Michael Ventris and Jean-François Champollion. Turing famously cracked the German Enigma code during World War II, Ventris decoded the Mycenaean Greek script called Linear B, and Champollion began to make sense of Egyptian Hieroglyphics, which had been a closed book to scholars for centuries.

There are some striking similarities between two of the Englishmen mentioned above: like James Prinsep, Michael

Ventris, who died in a motor accident in 1956 at the age of thirty-four, was charming and popular, able to assimilate languages quickly, and seemed to find time to turn a hobby into a serious contribution to the world's knowledge-base, despite working hard through World War II, and then pursuing a career as an architect. Prinsep was an important architect as well, and also a scientist, who came up with a practical method for measuring the temperature inside furnaces. Like Ventris, Prinsep also died young, in his case not because of an accident, but, in the opinion of some commentators, due to overwork: Champollion may also have died because of exhaustion.

Jean-François Champollion famously used a damaged inscribed rock called the Rosetta Stone to decode Egyptian Hieroglyphics. The Stone, which is now in the British Museum in London, includes parts of an identical inscription in Greek, Hieroglyphics, and Demotic, the cursive form of Ancient Egyptian writing. Put simply, once he had worked out what sounds the Hieroglyphic symbols represented, by comparing how the names of certain people were written in the Stone's three alphabets, Champollion was able to understand the underlying Ancient Egyptian words, because they were written in a language resembling Coptic, which he already knew. Poring over his Brahmi inscriptions, Princep, building on the work of others, was likewise able to make educated guesses at the sounds each character represented, and determined that they had been used to write in Prakrit, an ancient Indian language related to the better-known Sanskrit.

Although its unwitting role in unlocking the civilisation of the Ancient Egyptians cannot be denied, it must be said that, once translated, the text repeated on the Rosetta Stone is of little interest to non-specialists. It spends a lot of time on the inevitable but somewhat dull subject of taxation, and otherwise attempts to present a picture of the Egyptian royal family of the time as powerful, pious and efficient.

By contrast, the picture that emerged from some of the Brahmi inscriptions nineteenth-century scholars could read thanks to Prinsep's work was remarkable and unique. They spoke of an ancient Indian emperor called Devanampriya Priyardarsin (a name meaning 'beloved of the gods' and 'humane' or 'compassionate') who was powerful and victorious in battle, but felt remorse following his greatest military victory, and set about re-building his empire on a humane, Buddhism-inspired basis.

In Priyadarsin's imperial utopia, as revealed in the inscriptions, the emperor worked hard to ensure that justice was dispensed justly and disease countered with newly-built hospitals and newly-planted gardens of medicinal herbs. Education became more widespread, and everything was geared towards a general increase in health, happiness, enlightenment and piety.

Although Priyadarsin was keen to promote Buddhism, his so-called Edicts insisted on tolerance of the various Indian sects, and respect for their leaders and prophets. In this shiny new state, even animals would be treated kindly: Priyadarsin laid down that some should not be killed at all, that all should be exempt from torture, maiming and other forms of cruelty during life, and that far fewer should be killed as pious sacrifices.

At first, James Prinsep puzzled over exactly who this royal paragon, Priyadarsin, was. He guessed that he might have been a Sri Lankan king; but his colleague George Turnour, working in Sri Lanka itself, turned up evidence that Priyadarsin was the grandson of an earlier emperor called Chandragupta. He must therefore have been Ashoka Maurya, a figure who featured in Indian and Sri Lankan legends. (Ashoka is important to the Buddhists of Sri Lanka because they have traditionally believed that the emperor caused Buddhism to be brought to their island.)

Western scholars did not, however, have to resort to ancient Indian legends and other eastern texts to find out about Ashoka's grandfather, Chandragupta. The Greek historian Megasthenes, who probably died around 290 BCE, had served as an ambassador at the court of Chandragupta, whom he called Sandracottus in his writings on India.

The link between Chandragupta and Ashoka enabled researchers to connect the characters and events from ancient India that they were now learning about, to dates in western history. This was possible because of the areas to the north-west of modern India that had come under Greek influence after Alexander the Great invaded India in 326 BCE. Continuing contacts between the Greek and Indian worlds are also attested by some of the contents of the Ashoka inscriptions: Ashoka's edicts mention Hellenistic rulers such as Ptolemy II, then King of Egypt, and the Macedonian King Antigonus II Gonatas.

The new information about an ancient Indian civilisation with western contacts that had been revealed by nineteenth-century European colonisers appeared at a crucial time in the relationship between India and her new masters the British. The idea that India could have a history and literature that was impressive and inspiring ran counter to the notions of the 'Anglicisers' of the time, who stated that Indians would be better off if they forgot their own culture and embraced that of the west. In his shameful *Minute on Indian Education*, published in 1835, the English historian Thomas Babington Macaulay characterised Indian history as 'abounding with kings thirty feet high and reigns thirty thousand years long' and, moving on to Indian literature, he claimed that 'a single shelf of a good European library was worth the whole native literature of India and Arabia'.

In his *Minute*, Macaulay suggested that the (in his view) superior wonders of European literature would serve Indians much as the classical literature and history of Greek and

Rome served elite Europeans, who studied such texts in schools and colleges.

Macaulay's heroes among the literate Greeks and Romans would not, of course, have agreed with him about the inferiority of eastern culture. As Josephine Crawley Quinn pointed out in a recent article in the *Times Literary Supplement*, the Greeks and Romans were well aware that they lived to the west and north of some very advanced civilizations, and enthusiastically helped themselves to literary, legal, scientific, technological, artistic, architectural, religious and philosophical ideas from the Egyptians, the Phoenicians, the Persians and the Indians, among others (see *TLS* 21/09/18).

The ancient European view of eastern ideas is more in tune with the views of enlightened twenty-first century westerners than those of the blinkered, jingoistic Macaulay. There are now many white, English-speaking followers of Buddhism, the ancient religion Ashoka helped to promote, but which less than one percent of Indians now follow. Inspired by the contemporary Buddhism of places like Japan and Tibet, even people who would not dream of becoming Buddhists read classic Buddhist texts in translation, display Buddhist arts and crafts in their homes, practice Buddhist-style meditation, entertain ideas about reincarnation, listen to recordings of the chants of Buddhist monks, and even use Buddhist words like *Dharma* in everyday conversation. Beyond the Buddhist world, white British people in particular marry people of Indian heritage, watch Bollywood films, listen to both modern and traditional Indian music, and frequent Indian restaurants, many of which are named after Ashoka.

The rediscovery of the 'real', as opposed to the legendary, Ashoka by British investigators, including James Prinsep, must be counted as one of the gifts of the British to India, a sub-continent that they generally *took from* rather than *gave to*. As used by Nehru and others, the facts about Ashoka comprise an argument to use against those who still feel that people of white European heritage have always been superior to the black and brown people of the south and east. For those of us who feel, as H.G. Wells did, that we all belong to one race, the story of Ashoka is a universal story about the best of human possibilities.

SW, Durham, November 2018

James Prinsep; drawing by Colesworthy Grant

H.G. Wells

Other Histories, Other Worlds

Today H.G. Wells (1866-1946) is remembered as a writer of science fiction stories such as the novella *The Time Machine* (1895) and the novel *The War of the Worlds* (1898); but he also wrote realistic fiction, and non-fiction. His *Outline of History*, first published in book form in 1920, was an immense commercial success, and had a considerable influence on how its readers understood their planet and its past.

The fact that Wells included Ashoka in his *Outline* shows that he was determined to make his a genuine history of the whole world, not just a history of Europe or, worse, Britain, with occasional forays into the histories of other countries and continents. That he accords Ashoka special status as a uniquely virtuous monarch chimes in with his approach to the world's different races and nationalities in his *Outline*: he surprised many of its early readers by refusing to accept the idea that humanity consisted of any more than one race, asserted that all the so-called 'races' were more or less mixed, and stated that the idea of the superiority of the western mind 'dissolves into thin air' upon close examination.

Wells's striking statement that Ashoka was 'the only military monarch on record who abandoned warfare after victory' does not exactly 'dissolve' on close examination, but it certainly demands to be examined closely. The fact is that until relatively recently all monarchs were 'military monarchs', at least in theory. The last British monarch to participate in a battle as king was George II at the Battle of Dettingen in 1743, and Napoleon III of France fought at the Battle of Sedan in 1870. The history of East Anglia in the Anglo-Saxon period provides us with two examples of 'military monarchs' who gave up war, a decision which unfortunately led to the deaths of both of them. King Sigeberht died in 634 CE when he was forced into a battle against the Mercians: having embraced peace, he refused to arm himself, went into battle bearing only a staff, and was cut down. Some two centuries later, the royal saint King Edmund was killed by Vikings, partly because he had renounced war.

Ashoka iron pillar at Delhi, as shown in
Wells' *Outline of History*

From H.G. Wells,
Outline of History, 1920

The cult and doctrine of Gautama, gathering corruptions and variations from Brahminism and Hellenism alike, was spread throughout India by an increasing multitude of teachers in the fourth and third centuries b.c. For some generations at least it retained much of the moral beauty and something of the simplicity of the opening phase. Many people who have no intellectual grasp upon the meaning of self-abnegation and disnterestedness have nevertheless the ability to appreciate a splendour in the reality of these qualities. Early Buddhism was certainly producing noble lives, and it is not only through reason that the latent response to nobility is aroused in our minds. It spread rather in spite of than because of the concessions that it made to vulgar imaginations. It spread because many of the early Buddhists were sweet and gentle, helpful and noble and admirable people, who compelled belief in their sustaining faith.

Quite early in its career Buddhism came into conflict with the growing pretensions of the Brahmins. As we have already noted, this priestly caste was still only struggling to dominate Indian life in the days of Gautama. They had already great advantages. They had the monopoly of tradition and religious sacrifices. But their power was being challenged by the development of kingship, for the men who became clan leaders and kings were usually not of the Brahminical caste.

Kingship received an impetus from the Persian and Greek invasions of the Punjab. We have already noted the name of King Porus whom, in spite of his elephants, Alexander defeated and turned into a satrap. There came also to the Greek camp upon the Indus a certain adventurer named Chandragupta Maurya, whom the Greeks called Sandracottus, with a scheme for conquering the Ganges country. The scheme was not welcome to the Macedonians, who were in revolt against marching any further into India, and he had to fly the camp. He wandered among the tribes upon the north-west frontier, secured their support, and after Alexander had departed, overran the Punjab, ousting the Macedonian representatives. He then conquered the Ganges country (321 b.c.), waged a successful war (303 b.c.) against Seleueus (Seleucus I) when the latter attempted to recover the Punjab, and consolidated a great empire reaching across all the plain of northern India from the western to the eastern sea. And this King Chandragupta came into much the same conflict with the growing power of the Brahmins, into the conflict between crown and priesthood, that we have already noted as happening in Babylonia and Egypt and China. He saw in the spreading doctrine of Buddhism an ally against the growth of priestcraft and caste. He supported and endowed the Buddhistic Order, and encouraged its teachings.

He was succeeded by his son, who conquered Madras and was in turn succeeded by Ashoka (264 to 227 b.c.), one of the great monarchs of history, whose dominions extended from Afghanistan to Madras. He is the only military monarch on record who abandoned warfare after victory. He had invaded Kalinga (255 b.c.), a country along the east coast of Madras, perhaps with some intention of completing the conquest of the tip of the Indian peninsula. The expedition was successful, but he was disgusted by what he saw of the cruelties and horrors of war. He declared, in certain inscriptions that still exist, that he would no longer seek conquest by war, but by religion, and the rest of his life was devoted to the spreading of Buddhism throughout the world.

He seems to have ruled his vast empire in peace and with great ability. He was no mere religious fanatic. But in the year of his one and only war he joined the Buddhist community as a layman, and some years later he became a full member of the Order, and devoted himself to the attainment of Nirvana by the Eightfold Path. How entirely compatible that way of living then was with the most useful and beneficent activities his life shows. Right Aspiration, Right Effort, and Right Livelihood distinguished his career. He organized a great digging of wells in India, and the planting of trees for shade. He appointed officers for the supervision of charitable works. He founded hospitals and public gardens. He had gardens made for the growing of medicinal herbs. Had he had an Aristotle to inspire him, he would no doubt have endowed scientific research upon a great scale. He created a ministry for the care of the aborigines and subject races. He made provision for the education of women. He made, he was the first monarch to make, an attempt to educate his people into a common view of the ends and way of life. He made vast benefactions to the Buddhist teaching orders, and tried to stimulate them to a better study of their own literature. All over the land he set up long inscriptions rehearsing the teaching of Gautama, and it is the simple and human teaching and not the preposterous accretions. Thirty-five of his inscriptions survive to this day. Moreover, he sent missionaries to spread the noble and reasonable teaching of his master throughout the world, to Kashmir, to Ceylon, to the Seleucids, and the Ptolemies. It was one of these missions which carried that cutting of the Bo Tree, of which we have already told, to Ceylon.

For eight and twenty years Ashoka worked sanely for the real needs of men. Amidst the tens of thousands of names of monarchs that crowd the columns of history, their majesties and graciousnesses and serenities and royal highnesses and the like, the name of Ashoka shines, and shines almost alone, a star. From the Volga to Japan his name is still honoured. China, Tibet, and even India, though it has left his doctrine, preserve the tradition of his greatness. More living men cherish his memory to-day than have ever heard the names of Constantine or Charlemagne.

It is thought that the vast benefactions of Ashoka finally corrupted Buddhism by attracting to its Order great numbers of mercenary and insincere adherents, but there can be no doubt that its rapid extension throughout Asia was very largely due to his stimulus.

Prinsep's Ghat in Kolkata, photo by Grantidez

The Eminent Indologist

We can get some idea of the spirit in which Vincent Arthur Smith pursued his study of India by listening to part of a speech he gave on the subject of the Indian Civil Service, in which he had served for many years, at Trinity College Dublin in 1903:

There are diversities of gifts; and the duties of the Indian Civil Service are so diverse that there is room for men of all tastes — for the scholar as well as for the sportsman. The Indian Empire is a vast ethnological and linguistic museum, stored with an infinite treasure of materials for the study of the science of man in all its branches. The history and antiquities of the country offer an illimitable field for investigation; and I can testify from personal experience that these subjects can furnish welcome relaxation from official toil and ample occupation for the long leisure of retirement. I would earnestly desire to impress on all young officers going to India the necessity — I am tempted to say the duty — of acquiring and keeping at least one hobby. In the long hours of a day in the hot weather, when the offices happen to be closed, and nothing disturbs the deadly silence of the darkened house, when tobacco ceases to charm, and the delights of long drinks must be chastened with discretion — the man with a hobby may still be content and rejoice in the quiet which bores to death his idle comrade. Let the hobby be what it may — beetles, coins, postage-stamps, or anything — a man should see that he has one, and not be happy until he gets it.

Although these words from his lecture, which was frankly designed to encourage his young listeners to join the Indian Civil Service, may suggest that Smith was a dilettante, he was in fact a genuine scholar who did valuable work on the history, art and antiquities of India, and wrote books on these subjects in a lively, accessible style.

If Vincent Smith had gone out to India at the request of a native prince to work as a civil servant for him, his view of the country as 'a vast ethnological and linguistic museum' might not make for such unsettling reading for modern readers. The fact that, however studious, efficient and well-meaning he may have been, Vincent was just another British Smith sent out to stand on the neck of India makes his words disturbing. That he and his colleagues also found ample time for relaxation and even boredom in this role also leaves a bad taste in the mouth.

However dubious his attitude was in some respects, Smith's 1901 book on Ashoka, from which the following extracts have been taken, is engrossing and well-judged, and sits alongside his later volume on the Mughal emperor Akbar (1917).

For a complete modern account of one version of the Indian legend of Ashoka, the reader should turn to John S. Strong's 1983 book *The Legend of Ashoka*. Strong's work is arranged around a translation of the Ashokavadana, a Buddhist legend which was written down in the second century CE. Vincent Smith contents himself with *re-telling* the legends of the Buddhist king from the Sri Lankan and Indian traditions: he does not translate them word for word.

Although he re-tells them, Smith is scornful about the ancient Sri Lankan legends concerning Ashoka, saying that:

All the forms of those stories which have reached us are crowded with absurdities and contradictions from which legitimate criticism cannot extract trustworthy history . . . the undeserved credit given to the statements of the monks of Ceylon has been a great hindrance to the right understanding of ancient Indian history.

In his Ashoka book, Smith goes on to say that 'the [Sri Lankan] story of the mission of Mahendra and his sister . . . is a tissue of absurdities,' but, as we know, the aforementioned George Turnour, Sri Lanka's answer to James Prinsep, used evidence from the most ancient of these chronicles, the Dipavamsa, to prove that the leader whose personality dominates the Edicts of Ashoka was indeed Ashoka himself. Turnour also translated the Mahavamsa, an epic poem of Sri Lankan history that was written around the sixth century CE. The Mahavamsa is another important source of information on Ashoka.

Together with the edicts that Ashoka left scattered all over his empire, the legends of Ashoka are one of the two main sources of information that we have about this remarkable Indian. The legends were, however, written down later than the edicts, most of which were probably made, or at least commissioned, when Ashoka was still alive.

In the nature of legends, those dealing with Ashoka were probably fossilised as text after a long period of evolution in the oral narrative tradition that is still strong in India. Over time, elements of the 'original' story would no doubt have vanished or been transformed, and new, spurious elements would have attached themselves to the original core story. The result is that the picture of Ashoka that we get from the legends, at least as re-told by Vincent Smith, is different from the impression we get from the edicts. The most striking difference concerns Ashoka's tragic war against the Kalingas. This does not appear in the legends: Ashoka is converted into a pious, compassionate ruler not by post-war remorse but by the influence of Buddhist saints whom he encounters once he has gained power by highly suspect means.

Writers like Carl Jung, Northrop Frye and Joseph Campbell, author of the influential *Hero With A Thousand Faces* (1949) have pointed out how enduring mythical or legendary stories tend to contain certain archetypal elements that seem to be common to such stories in many cultures. Modern users of Campbell's work in particular have shown how these elements can re-surface in unlikely places, giving a kind of mythic power to unlikely sorts of narratives, such as children's cartoons, fairy-stories and science-fiction films.

An element that the legends of Ashoka share with other mythical tales is the wicked step-mother, in this case the emperor's youthful second wife Tishyarakshita, described as 'dissolute and unprincipled'. Her inappropriate passion for her step-son Kunala leads to all sorts of trouble, as does Phaedra's passion for her step-son Hippolytus in Greek mythology. In the Old Testament, Potiphar's wife, who lusts after the virtuous Joseph, is a similar character. Another tragically unsuitable attachment is that of the Greek King Oedipus for Jocasta, who of course turns out to be his mother. In ancient Egyptian literature, there is also *The Story of Two Brothers*, in which a woman lusts after her brother-in-law, with unfortunate results.

Mythical heroes from the ancient world often enjoy super-human powers and/or a special link to the divine world. Greek heroes and heroines are often closely related to immortal gods or goddesses, and in the Judeo-Christian tradition characters like King David are especially favoured by God, and seem to have an instinctive understanding of what he requires of them.

Although he is immensely powerful in his youth, able to see across vast distances and summon genii to do his bidding, the Ashoka of the legends becomes pitifully powerless as an old man, when he finds that his orders are simply not being carried out: this is reminiscent of Shakespeare's King Lear. The fact that Ashoka's shrinking power is associated with his attachment to an alluring but unsuitable woman also reminds us of Antony in Shakespeare's *Antony and Cleopatra*.

The details of Ashoka's lamentable position in later life closely resemble the features of myths of the 'autumnal' phase of human existence, as classified by the Canadian theorist Northrop Frye. In his *Archetypes of Literature* (1951) Frye suggests that in his autumnal phase the archetypal mythical hero often faces imminent death without friends: his companions are typically a traitor, and a siren or temptress.

The pitiful picture, presented in the Indian legend, of Ashoka's unfortunate son Kunala wandering around as a blind beggar, accompanied only by his faithful wife, is reminiscent of the character of Gloucester in *King Lear*, and Oedipus in Sophocles' play *Oedipus at Colonus*. In the latter, the aforementioned king of Thebes, who has blinded himself out of guilt for his incestuous passion for his mother, ultimately meets with compassionate treatment, as does Kunala in the legend of Ashoka.

It is often said that a true hero must have at least one weakness. The archetypal comic-book hero Superman has his kryptonite, the Agamemnon of Greek tragedy is weakened by pride or hubris, and in his book *The Basic Formulas of Fiction* William Foster Harris argues that the U.S. president Theodore Roosevelt would make a perfect hero because, with all his excellent qualities, he suffered from terrible eyesight.

Early in the Ashoka legends we learn that the hero's life is blighted by the curse of ugliness. This causes him to become something of an outcast, treated with contempt both by his relatives and the women of the royal court. If one were writing an intense, psychological novel about Ashoka, one might be tempted to link his ugliness to his misplaced affection for the scheming Tishyarakshita.

In later life, the eminent Indologist Vincent Arthur Smith misused his status as a respected historian of India to argue that the Indians could not rule their own country democratically, much as that other historian, T.B. Macaulay, had argued that the history and literature of the Indians was not worth teaching. In a book published to argue against proposed reforms that would have given the natives a greater role in the government of their own country, Smith gave his opinion that the 'notions' of 'advanced reformers':

. . . run counter to a deep stream of Indian tradition which has been flowing for thousands of years. Ninety-nine out of a hundred Indians, whether Hindus or Muhammadans, cherish as their ideal of government that of the virtuous Raja, who works hard, is easily accessible, is sternly and impartially just, yet loves his people as a father loves his children, and is guided by the advice of wise ministers based upon immemorial tradition. Executive weakness, unjust partiality, and departure from tradition are regarded with substantial unanimity as among the worst possible faults of a government.

(from *Indian Constitutional Reform Viewed by the Light of History*, 1919)

Confident, it seems, that his readers in 1919 would need no introduction to the figure of Ashoka, Smith cites 'the declarations of Ashoka' that he had written about nearly twenty years earlier as proof of ordinary Indians' traditional devotion to the idea of an all-powerful monarch who is also a tireless servant of his people. Smith suggests that, for the Indians of his time, the figure of the king of England should continue to serve as the focus for their instinctive loyalty. Referring to George V's visit to India in 1911, Smith suggests that:

> . . . the now acknowledged supremacy of the Crown offers an opportunity for the exhibition of the traditional Indian loyalty to a person, which should be sedulously kept open. The Indian people have enjoyed the privilege of seeing face to face their King-Emperor, the successor of Rama, Ashoka, and Akbar. Their heartfelt loyalty should not be quenched by the cold water of democratic theory.

It would seem from these statements of Smith's that he was overcome by a nostalgic sense of some glittering, golden era of India's past, such as the period reigned over by Ashoka, and dreamed that the British could restore something like the spirit of that time to their short-lived Raj. In any case, Smith's apparent inability to see the Indians among whom he lived for five decades as anything other than hidebound fools does not contradict, and may even be closely related to, his genuine enthusiasm for Ashoka and his story.

I have made slight adaptations to Smith's re-tellings of the Sri Lankan and Indian legends of Ashoka to aid readability, but without, I hope, compromising the meaning Smith hoped to convey. I hope readers will find it interesting to compare the mainland and island versions, which do not agree.

In places, Smith offers us alternative versions of the same story from the Indian tradition, and in other places his stories seem to contradict each other, for instance in his account of the Indian legends, where in one place Ashoka's wicked second queen appears to be extremely active, although she has just been burned alive in the previous story. Like many legends from different cultures, those concerning Ashoka are episodic, and cannot honestly be strung together into a coherent, consistent narrative, like that to be found in a popular novel. Their characteristic lack of a unifying

thread of narrative is one aspect that makes critical readers
of such stories suspect that some may have been imported
from other sources and added to a core set of stories as
spurious embellishments.

Ashoka and his queen – relief at Sanchi,
Madhya Pradesh. Photo by Biswarup Ganguly

The Sri Lankan Legend of Ashoka

Kalasoka, king of Magadha, had ten sons, who after his death ruled the kingdom righteously for twenty-two years. They were succeeded by other nine brothers, the Nandas, who likewise, in order of seniority, ruled the kingdom for twenty-two years. A Brahman named Chanakya, who had conceived an implacable hatred against Dhana Nanda, the last survivor of the nine brothers, put that king to death, and placed upon the throne Chandra Gupta, a member of the princely Maurya clan, who assumed the sovereignty of all India, and reigned gloriously for twenty-four years. He was succeeded by his son Bindusara, who ruled the land for twenty-eight years.

The sons of Bindusara, the offspring of sixteen mothers, numbered one hundred and one, of whom the eldest was named Sumana, and the youngest Tishya. A third son, Ashoka, uterine brother of Tishya, had been appointed Viceroy of Western India by his father. On receiving news of King Bindusara's mortal illness, Ashoka quitted Ujjain, the seat of his government, and hastened to Pataliputra (Patna), the capital of the empire. On his arrival at the capital, he slew his eldest brother Sumana, and ninety-eight other brothers, saving alive but one, Tishya, the youngest of all. Having thus secured his throne, Ashoka became lord of all India, but by reason of the massacre of his brothers he was known as Ashoka the Wicked.

Now it so happened that when Prince Sumana was slain,

his wife was with child. She fled from the slaughter, and was obliged to seek shelter in a village of outcastes beyond the eastern gate. The headman of the outcastes, pitying her misery, entreated her kindly, and, doing her reverence, served her faithfully for seven years. On that very day on which she was driven forth from the palace she gave birth to a boy, on whom the name Nigrodha was bestowed. The child was born with the marks of sanctity, and when he attained the age of seven was already an ordained monk.

The holy child, whose royal origin was not known, happened one day to pass by the palace, and attracted the attention of the king, who was struck by his grave and reverend deportment. King Ashoka, highly delighted, sent for the boy, who drew near with decorum and self-possession.

The king said, 'My child, take any seat which thou thinkest befitting.' Nigrodha, seeing that no priest other than himself was present, advanced towards the royal throne as the befitting seat. Whereupon King Ashoka, understanding that this monk was destined to become lord of the palace, gave the boy his arm, and seating him upon the throne, refreshed him with meat and drink prepared for his own royal use.

Having thus shown his respect, the king questioned the boy monk concerning the doctrines of Buddha, and received from him an exposition of the doctrine of earnestness, to the effect that earnestness is the way to immortality, indifference is the way to death. This teaching so wrought upon the heart of the king, that he at once accepted the religion of Buddha, and gave gifts to the priesthood. The next day Nigrodha returned to the palace with thirty-two priests, and, by preaching the law, established king and people in the faith and the practice of piety. In this manner was King Ashoka constrained to abandon the Brahmanical faith of his father, and to accept as a lay disciple the sacred law of Buddha.

These things happened in the fourth year after the

accession of King Ashoka, who in the same year celebrated his solemn coronation, and appointed his younger brother Tishya to be his deputy or vicegerent.

The sixty thousand Brahmans, who for three years had daily enjoyed the bounty of Ashoka, as they had enjoyed that of his predecessors on the throne, were dismissed, and in their place Buddhist monks in equal numbers were constantly entertained at the palace, and treated with such lavish generosity that four lakhs of treasure were each day expended. One day, the king, having feasted the monks at the palace, inquired the number of the sections of the law, and having learned that the sections of the law were eighty-four thousand in number, he resolved to dedicate a sacred edifice to each. Wherefore, the king commanded the local rulers to erect eighty-four thousand sacred edifices in as many towns of India, and himself constructed the Ashokarama at the capital. All the edifices were completed within three years, and in a single day the news of their completion reached the Court. By means of the supernatural powers with which he was gifted, King Ashoka was enabled to behold at one glance all these works throughout the empire.

From the time of his consecration as emperor of India, two hundred and eighteen years after the death of the perfect Buddha, the miraculous faculties of royal majesty entered into King Ashoka, and the glory which he obtained by his merit extended a league above and a league below the earth.

The denizens of heaven were his servants, and daily brought for his use water from the holy lake, luscious, fragrant fruits, and other good things beyond measure and without stint.

The king, lamenting that he had been born too late to behold the Buddha in the flesh, besought the aid of the Snake-King, who caused to appear a most enchanting image of Buddha, in the full perfection of beauty, surrounded by a halo of glory, and surmounted by the lambent flame of sanctity, in honour of which glorious vision a magnificent festival was held for the space of seven days.

While Ashoka during his royal father's lifetime was stationed at Ujjain as viceroy of the Avanti country, he formed a connexion with a lady of the Setthi caste, named Devi, who resided at Yedisagiri (Besnagar near Bhilsa). She accompanied the prince to Ujjain, and there bore to him a son named Mahendra, two hundred and four years after the death of Buddha. Two years later a daughter named Sanghamitra was born. Devi continued to reside at Vedisagiri after Ashoka seized the throne; but the children accompanied their father to the capital, where Sanghamitra was given in marriage to Agni Brahma, nephew of the king, to whom she bore a son named Sumana.

In the fourth year after King Ashoka's coronation, his brother Tishya, the vicegerent, his nephew Agni Brahma, and his grandson Sumana were all ordained. The king, who had received the news of the completion of the eighty-four thousand sacred edifices, held a solemn assembly of millions of monks and nuns, and, coming in full state in person, took up his station in the midst of the priesthood. The king's piety had by this time washed away the stain of fratricide, and he who had been known as Ashoka the Wicked, was henceforth celebrated as Ashoka the Pious.

After his brother Tishya had devoted himself to religion, Ashoka proposed to replace him in the office of vicegerent by Prince Mahendra, but at the urgent entreaty of his spiritual director, Tishya son of Moggali (Mudgalya), the king was persuaded to permit of the ordination both of Mahendra and his sister Sanghamitra. The young prince had then attained the canonical age of twenty, and was therefore at once ordained. The princess assumed the yellow robe, but was obliged to defer her admission to the Order for two years, until she should attain full age. Mahendra was ordained in the sixth year of the king's reign, dating from his coronation.

In the eighth year of the reign, two saints, named respectively Sumitra and Tishya, died. Their death was attended with such portents that the world at large became greatly devoted to the Buddhist religion, and the liberality of the people to the priests was multiplied. The profits so obtained attracted to the Order many unworthy members, who set up their own doctrines as the doctrines of Buddha, and performed unlawful rites and ceremonies, even sacrifices after the manner of the Brahmans, as seemed good unto them. Hence was wrought confusion both in the doctrine and ritual of the Church.

The disorders waxed so great that the heretics outnumbered the true believers, the regular rites of the church were in abeyance for seven years, and the king's spiritual director, Tishya son of Moggali, was obliged to commit his disciples to the care of Prince Mahendra, and himself to retire into solitude among the mountains at the source of the Ganges.

Tishya, the son of Moggali, having been persuaded to quit his retreat, expelled the heretics, produced the Kathavatthu treatise, and held the Third Council of the Church at the Ashokarama in Pataliputra. These events happened in the year two hundred and thirty-six after the death of Buddha, and seventeen and a half years after the coronation of King Ashoka.

In the same year King Devanampiya Tissa (Tishya) ascended the throne of Ceylon, and became the firm friend and ally of King Ashoka, although the two sovereigns never met. The King of Ceylon, in order to show his friendship and respect, dispatched a mission to India, headed by his nephew, Maha Arittha. In seven days the envoys reached the port of Tamalipti (Tamluk in Bengal), and in seven days more arrived at the Imperial Court. They were royally entertained by King Ashoka, who was graciously pleased to accept the rich and rare presents sent by his ally, in return for which he sent gifts of equal value. The envoys remained at the capital for five months, and then returned to the island by the way they had come, bearing to their sovereign this message from King Ashoka: 'I have taken refuge in the Buddha, the Law, and the Order; I have avowed myself a lay disciple of the doctrine of the son of the Sakyas. Imbue your mind also with faith in this Triad, in the highest religion of the Jina; take refuge in the Teacher.'

After the close of the Third Council, which remained in session for nine months, Tishya the son of Moggali resolved that the law of Buddha should be communicated to foreign countries, and dispatched missionaries to Kashmir and Gandhara; to Mahisamandala (Mysore); to Vanavasi (North Kanara); to Aparantaka (coast north of Bombay); to Maharashtra; to the Yavana country (on the north-western frontier); to the mountain regions of the Himalaya; to Suvarnablhumi (Pegu); and to Ceylon.

The mission to Ceylon consisted of Prince Mahendra and five colleagues, of whom one was Sumana, his sister's son.

Mahendra resolved, with the king's permission, to visit his mother and her relations on his way to Ceylon, and devoted six months to this purpose.

He found his mother at her home in Yedisagiri, and, having been received with great joy, was accommodated in the splendid monastery at that place which she had erected. The preaching of Mahendra converted Bhandu, a grandnephew of his mother. After this event Mahendra lingered for another month, and then with his companions, to whom Bhandu attached himself, rose aloft into the air, and flying, 'as flies the king of swans' arrived in Ceylon, and alighted upon the Missa mountain.

The first discourse pronounced by the leader of the mission converted the king, with forty thousand of his followers. The princess Anula, with five hundred of her attendants, desired to enter the Order, but was told that the male missionaries had no power to ordain females, who, however, might be ordained by the princess Sanghamitra.

The king of Ceylon, after due deliberation, again dispatched his nephew to King Ashoka, with instructions to bring back Sanghamitra and a branch of the sacred bo-tree. King Ashoka, although grieving sorely at the separation from his beloved daughter, gave his consent to her deputation to Ceylon, and proceeded with much ceremony to sever a branch of the holy tree.

The severance was effected, signalized by many miracles, and the envoys, accompanied by Sanghamitra, were dispatched to the port of Tamalipti, escorted by an army commanded by King Ashoka in person.

The vessel in which the bo-tree was embarked briskly dashed through the water; and in the great ocean, through the circumference of a league, the waves were stilled; flowers of the five different colours blossomed around it, and various melodies of music rang in the air. The holy branch, thus miraculously wafted to the shore of the island, was received with due honour, and was planted in the Mahamegha garden, which the king had dedicated to the use of the Order. The branch threw off eight vigorous shoots, which were distributed and planted in as many localities.

In those days also the king of Ceylon built for Mahendra the Mahavihara, the first monastery of the island, and the construction of the Chetiyagiri (Mihintale) monastery followed soon after.

The princess Anula, in company with five hundred virgins and five hundred women of the palace, was duly ordained as a nun by Sanghamitra, and straightway attained the rank of Arhat. The king erected a nunnery for Sanghamitra, who there abode in peace, until she died in the fifty-ninth year after her ordination, that being the ninth year of the reign of the Ceylonese King Uttiyaa. Her brother Mahendra had passed away in the previous year, while observing the sixtieth retreat since his ordination.

While King Ashoka was engaged in the festivals connected with the dispatch of the branch of the bo-tree, another mission, headed by his grandson Sumana, arrived from Ceylon to beg for relics to be enshrined in the great stupa by the island king. The request of this second mission also was granted by King Ashoka, who bestowed upon his ally a dishful of holy relics, to which Sakra, lord of the Devas, added the right collar-bone of Buddha, extracted from the Chulamani stupa. The relics were received with extreme honour, and enshrined with due ceremony in the Thuparama stupa, the moment being marked by a terrific earthquake. Witnessing this miracle, the people were converted in crowds, and the king's younger brother joined the Order, which in those days received an accession of thirty thousand monks.

When, as has been related, the heretics waxed great in numbers and wrought confusion in the Church, so that for seven years the rite of confession and other solemn rites remained in abeyance, King Ashoka determined that the disorder should cease, and sent a minister to the Ashokarama to compel the monks to resume the services. The minister, having gone there, assembled the monks and proclaimed the royal commands. The holy men replied that they could not perform the services while the heretics remained. Thereupon the minister, exceeding his instructions, with his own hand smote off the heads of several of the contumacious ecclesiastics as they sat in convocation. The king's brother Tishya interfered, and prevented further violence.

The king was profoundly horrified and greatly alarmed at the rash act of his minister, and sought absolution. In accordance with the advice of the clergy, the aged Tishya, son of Moggali, was summoned from his distant retreat, and conveyed by boat down the Ganges to the capital, where he was received by the king with extraordinary honour and reverence.

Ashoka, desiring to test the supernatural powers of the

saint, begged that a miracle might be performed, and specially requested that an earthquake confined to a limited space might be produced. The saint placed a chariot, a horse, a man, and a vessel filled with water, one on each side of a square space, exactly on the boundary lines, and produced an earthquake which caused the half of each object within the boundary line to quake, while the other half of each remained unshaken. Satisfied by this display of power, Ashoka inquired if the sacrilegious murder of the priests by the minister must be accounted as the king's sin. The saint ruled that where there is no wilful intention, there is no sin, and, accordingly, absolved Ashoka, whom he instructed fully in the truth.

The king commanded that all the priests in India, without exception, should be assembled, and taking his seat by the side of his spiritual director, examined each priest individually as to his faith. The saint decided that the doctrine of the Vaibadhyavadina school was the true primitive teaching of the master, and all dissenters were expelled, to the number of sixty thousand. A thousand orthodox priests of holy character were then selected to form a convocation or Council. To these assembled priests, Tishya, son of Moggali, recited the treatise called Kathavatthu in order to dissipate doubts on points of faith. The Council, following the procedure of the First Council at Rajagriha and the Second Council at Vaisali, recited and verified the whole body of the scriptures, and, after a session lasting nine months, dispersed. At the conclusion of the Council the earth quaked, as if to say 'Well done,' beholding the re-establishment of religion. Tishya, the son of Moggali, was then seventy-two years of age.

One day, Tishya, the younger brother of Ashoka, and Vicegerent of the empire, happened to be in a forest, and watched a herd of elk at play. The thought occurred to him that when elks browsing in the forest divert themselves, there seems to be no good reason why monks well lodged and well fed in monasteries should not amuse themselves. Coming home, the vicegerent told his thoughts to the king, who, in order to make him understand the reason why, conferred upon him the sovereignty for the space of seven days, saying, 'Prince, govern the empire for seven days, at the end of which I shall put thee to death.' At the close of the seventh day the king asked the prince: 'Why art thou grown so wasted?' He replied, 'By reason of the horror of death.' The king rejoined, 'Child, thou hast ceased to amuse thyself, because thou thinkest that in seven days thou wilt be put to death. These monks are meditating without ceasing on death; how then can they engage in frivolous diversions?'

The prince understood, and became a convert. Some time afterwards he was on a hunting expedition in the forest, when he saw the saint Mahadharmarakshita, a man of perfect piety and freed from the bonds of sin, sitting under a tree, and being fanned with a branch by an elephant. The prince, beholding this sight, longed for the time when he might become even as that saint and dwell at peace in the forest. The saint, in order to incline the heart of the prince unto the faith, soared into the air and alighted on the surface of the water of the Ashokarama tank, wherein he bathed, while his robes remained poised in the air. The prince was so delighted with this miracle that he at once resolved to become a monk, and begged the king for permission to receive ordination.

The king, being unwilling to thwart his pious desire, himself led the prince to the monastery, where ordination was conferred by the saint Mahadharmarakshita. At the same time one hundred thousand other persons were ordained, and no man can tell the number of those who became monks by reason of the example set by the prince.

The branch of the holy bo-tree, brought to Ceylon in the manner above related, was dispatched in the eighteenth year of the reign of Ashoka the Pious, and planted in the Mahameghavana garden in Ceylon.

In the twelfth year after that event, Asandhimitra, the beloved queen of Ashoka, who had shared his devotion to Buddhism, died. In the fourth year after her decease, the king, prompted by sensual passion, raised the princess Tishyarakshita to the dignity of queen-consort. She was young and vain, and very sensible of her personal charms. The king's devotion to the bo-tree seemed to her to be a slight to her attractions, and in the fourth year after her elevation her jealousy induced her to make an attempt to destroy the holy tree by magic. The attempt failed. In the fourth year after that event, King Ashoka the Pious fulfilled the lot of mortality, having reigned thirty-seven years.

Relief of Ashoka at Sanchi,
photo by Anandajoti Bhikkhu

The Indian Legends of Ashoka

King Bimbisara reigned at Raj agriha. His son was Ajatasatru, whose son was Udayibhadra, whose son was Munda, whose son was Kakavarnin, whose son was Sahalin, whose son was Tulakuchi, whose son was Mahamandala, whose son was Prasenajit, whose son was Nanda, whose son was Bindusara.

King Bindusara reigned at Pataliputra, and had a son named Susima.

A certain Brahman of Champa had a lovely daughter. A prophecy declared that she was destined to be the mother of two sons, of whom one would become universal monarch, and the other would attain the goal of the life of a recluse. The Brahman, seeking the fulfilment of the prophecy, succeeded in introducing his daughter into the palace, but the jealousy of the queens debarred her from the royal embraces, and assigned to her the menial duties of a barber. After some time the girl managed to explain to the king that she was no barber, but the daughter of a Brahman. When the king understood that she belonged to a caste with a member of which he could honourably consort, he at once took her into favour and made her chief queen. In due course, the Brahman's daughter, whose name was Subhadrangi, bore to the king two sons, the elder named Ashoka, and the younger named Vigatasoka.

The ascetic Pingala Vatsajiva, when consulted by King Bindusara concerning the destiny of the two boys, feared to tell his sovereign the truth, because Ashoka was rough-looking and displeasing in the sight of his father; but he frankly told Queen Subhadrangi that her son Ashoka was destined for the throne.

It came to pass that King Bindusara desired to besiege Taxila, which was in rebellion. The king ordered his despised son Ashoka to undertake the siege, and yet would not supply him with chariots or the needful munitions of war. Ill-supplied as he was, the prince obediently started to carry out the king's orders, whereupon the earth opened, and from her bosom supplied all his wants. When Ashoka with his army approached Taxila, the citizens came forth to meet him, protesting that their quarrel was only with oppressive ministers, not with the king or the king's son. Taxila and the kingdom of the Svasas made their submission to the prince, who in due course returned to the capital.

It came to pass that one day Prince Susima, the king's eldest son, was coming into the palace from the garden when he playfully threw his glove at the head of the prime minister Khallataka. The minister was deeply offended, and from that day engaged in a conspiracy with five hundred privy councillors to exclude Susima, and to place Ashoka on the throne.

The people of Taxila again revolted, and Prince Susima, who was deputed to reduce them to obedience, failed in his task. King Bindusara, who was then old and ill, desired to send Ashoka to Taxila, and to recall Susima, that he might take up the succession.

The ministers, however, continued to exclude the elder prince, and to secure the throne for Ashoka, on whose head the gods themselves placed the crown, at the moment when his father expired. Susima marched against Pataliputra, to assert his rights and expel the usurper; but Ashoka and his minister Radhagupta obtained the services of naked giants, who successfully guarded the gates, and by stratagem Susima was inveigled, so that he fell into a ditch full of burning fuel, and there miserably perished.

One day, when five hundred of his ministers ventured to resist the royal will, Ashoka, transported with rage, drew his sword, and with his own hand cut off the heads of all the offenders.

Another day, the women of the palace, whom Ashoka's rough features failed to please, mocked him by breaking off the leaves of an asoka tree in the garden. The king, when he heard of the incident, caused five hundred women to be burnt alive.

The ministers, horrified at these acts of cruelty, entreated the king not to defile his royal hands with blood, but to appoint an executioner to carry out sentences.

The king accepted this advice, and a man named Chandagirika, a wretch of unexampled cruelty, who loved to torture animals, and had slain his father and mother, was sought out and appointed Chief Executioner. For his use the king caused to be built a prison, which had a most attractive exterior, so that men might be tempted to enter it, and thus suffer all the tortures of hell which awaited them within; for the king had commanded that no man who entered this prison should leave it alive.

One day, a holy ascetic named Balapandita unwittingly entered the gate, and was instantly seized by the jailer. The holy man, though given seven days' respite, was at the end of the term of grace ruthlessly cast into a seething cauldron of filth, beneath which a great fire was kindled. The cruel jailer, looking in, beheld the saint, seated on a lotus, and unscathed by fire. The miracle having been reported to the palace, the king himself came to see it, and being converted by the sight and the preaching of the holy man, embraced the true religion and forsook the paths of wickedness.

The prison was demolished, and the jailer was burnt alive.

With the help of genii, Ashoka had thousands of stupas built all over his empire. By this time, the relics of the Buddha had been removed from the eight stupas where they had originally been enshrined. At the moment of a solar eclipse the genii, in obedience to the commands of the king, simultaneously deposited the relics in all the new stupas they had built.

The worshipful, the fortunate King Ashoka Maurya had caused the erection of all these stupas for the benefit of created beings; formerly he was called on earth Ashoka the Wicked, but this good work has earned for him the name of Ashoka the pious.

Having erected eighty-four thousand stupas, King Ashoka expressed a desire to visit the holy places of his religion. By the advice of his counsellors he sent for the saint Upagupta, son of Gupta the perfumer. Upagupta had been, in accordance with prophecy, born a century after the death of Buddha, and, when summoned by the king, was dwelling on Mount Urumunda in the Natabhatika forest near Mathura.

The saint accepted the royal invitation, and, accompanied by eighteen thousand holy men, travelled in state by boat down the Jumna and Ganges to Pataliputra, where he was received with the utmost reverence and honour.

The king said: 'I desire to visit all the places where the Venerable Buddha stayed, to do honour unto them, and to mark each with an enduring memorial for the instruction of the most remote posterity.' The saint approved of the project, and undertook to act as guide. Escorted by a mighty army, the monarch visited all the holy places in order.

The first place visited was the Lumbini Garden. Here Upagupta said: 'In this spot, great king, the Venerable One was born,' and added: 'Here is the first monument consecrated in honour of the Buddha, the sight of whom is excellent. Here, the moment after his birth, the recluse took seven steps upon the ground.'

The king bestowed a hundred thousand gold pieces on the people of the place, and built a stupa. He then passed on to Kapilavastu.

The royal pilgrim next visited the Bodhi-tree at Buddha Gaya, and there also gave a largess of a hundred thousand gold pieces, and built a chaitya. Eishipatana (Sarnath) near Benares, where Gautama had 'turned the wheel of the law,' and Kusinagara, where the Teacher had passed away, were also visited with similar observances. At Sravasti the pilgrims did reverence to the Jetavana monastery, where Gautama had so long dwelt and taught, and to the stupas of his disciples, Sariputra, Maudgalayana, and Maha Kasyapa. But when the king visited the stupa of Yakkula, he gave only one copper coin, inasmuch as Yakkula had met with few obstacles in the path of holiness, and had done little good to his fellow creatures. At the stupa of Ananda, the faithful attendant of Gautama, the royal gift amounted to six million gold pieces.

Yitasoka, the king's brother, was an adherent of the Tirthyas, who reproached the Buddhist monks as being men who loved pleasure and feared pain. Ashoka's efforts to convert his brother were met by the retort that the king was merely a tool in the hands of the monks. The king therefore resolved to effect his brother's conversion by stratagem.

At his instigation the ministers tricked Yitasoka into the assumption of the insignia of royalty. The king, when informed of what had happened, feigned great anger, and threatened his brother with instant death. Ultimately he was persuaded to grant the offender seven days' respite, and to permit him to exercise sovereign power during those seven days. During this period the fear of death so wrought upon the mind of Yitasoka that he embraced the doctrine of Buddha, in which he was instructed by the holy Sthavira Yasas. With difficulty the king was persuaded by the Sthavira Yasas to grant to his brother permission to become a monk. In order to initiate the novice gradually into the habits of the life of a mendicant friar, Ashoka prepared a hermitage for him within the palace grounds. From this hermitage Yitasoka withdrew, first to the Kukkutarama monastery, and afterwards to Yideha (Tirhut), where he attained to the rank of a saint (arhat). When Yitasoka, clad in rags, returned to the palace, he was received with great honour, and was induced to exhibit his supernatural powers. He then again withdrew to a distant retreat beyond the frontier, where he fell ill. Ashoka sent him medicine, and he recovered.

In those days it happened that a devoted adherent of the Brahman ascetics threw down and broke a statue of Buddha at Pundra Yardhana in Bengal. As a penalty for the sacrilege eighteen thousand inhabitants of that city were massacred in one day by order of Ashoka. Some time after, another fanatic at Pataliputra similarly overthrew a statue of Buddha. The persons concerned, with all their relatives and friends, were burned alive, and the king placed the price of a dindra on the head of every Brahmanical ascetic.

Now, when the proclamation was published Vitasoka, clad in his beggar's garb, happened to be lodging for the night in the hut of a cowherd. The good wife, seeing the unkempt and dishevelled appearance of her guest, was convinced that he must be one of the proclaimed ascetics, and persuaded her husband to slay him in order to earn the reward. The cowherd carried his victim's head to the king, who was horrified at the sight, and was persuaded by his ministers to revoke the proclamation. Not only did he revoke the cruel proclamation, but he gave the world peace by ordaining that henceforth no one should be put to death.

King Ashoka early in his reign had a half-brother, the son of his mother, who was younger than the king, and belonged to a noble family. The young man was extravagant, wasteful, and cruel in disposition. In his dress also he aped the royal costume.

The indignation of the people became so great that the ministers ventured to remonstrate with the king, and to say: 'Your majesty's brother in his pride assumes a dignity beyond his due. When the government is impartial, the subjects are contented; when the subjects are content, the sovereign is at peace. We desire that you should preserve the principles of government handed down to us by our fathers, and that you should deliver to justice the men who seek to change those principles.'

Then King Ashoka, weeping, addressed his brother and said: 'I have inherited from my ancestors the duty of protecting my people; how is it that you, my own brother, have forgotten my affection and kindness? It is impossible for me at the very beginning of my reign to disregard the laws. If I punish you, I dread the resentment of my ancestors; if I pass over your transgressions, I dread the ill opinion of my people.'

The prince, bowing his head, admitted his error, and begged for nothing more than a respite of seven days. The king granted this request, and threw his brother into a dark dungeon, though he provided him with exquisite food and all other luxuries. At the end of the first day the guard cried out to the prisoner: 'One day has gone; six days are left.' By the time the sixth day had expired, the prisoner's repentance and discipline were complete. He attained at once to the rank of a saint (arhat), and feeling conscious of miraculous powers, ascended into the air.

Ashoka went in person to the dungeon, and told his brother that having now, contrary to expectation, attained the highest degree of holiness, he might return to his place. Mahendra replied that he had lost all taste for the pleasures of the world, and desired to live in solitude. Ashoka consented, but pointed out that it was unnecessary for the prince to retire to the mountains, as a hermitage could be constructed at the capital. The king then caused the genii to build a stone house, as already related.

Mahendra, after his conversion, journeyed to the south of India, and built a monastery in the delta of the Kaveri (Cauvery), of which the ruins were still visible a thousand years later.

He is also related to have made use of his supernatural powers to pass through the air to Ceylon, in which island he spread the knowledge of the true law, and widely diffused the doctrine bequeathed to his disciples by the Master. From the time of Mahendra, the people of Ceylon, who had been addicted to a corrupt form of religion, forsook their ancient errors and heartily accepted the truth.

After the death of his faithful consort Asandhimitra, King Ashoka, late in life, married Tishyarakshita, a dissolute and unprincipled young woman. She cast amorous glances on her stepson Kunala, her worthy predecessor's son, who was famous for the beauty of his eyes. The virtuous prince rejected with horror the advances made by his stepmother, who then became filled with 'the spite of contemned beauty' and changed her hot love into bitter hate. In pursuance of a deep-laid scheme for the destruction of him who by his virtue had put her vice to shame, the queen with honied words persuaded the king to depute Kunala to the government of distant Taxila.

The prince obediently accepted the honourable commission, and when departing was warned by his father to verify orders received, which, if genuine, would be sealed with an impression of the king's teeth. The queen bided her time, with ever-growing hatred. After the lapse of some months she wrote a dispatch, addressed to the viceroy's ministers at Taxila, directing them immediately on receipt of the orders to put out the eyes of the viceroy, Prince Kunala, to lead him and his wife into the mountains, and to there leave them to perish.

She sealed the dispatch with royal red wax, and, when the king was asleep, furtively stamped the wax with the impression of his teeth, and sent off the orders with all speed to Taxila. The ministers who received the orders knew not what to do. The prince, noticing their confusion, compelled them to explain. The ministers wished to compromise by detaining the prince in custody, pending a reference to the capital. But the prince would not permit of any delay, and said: 'My father, if he has ordered my death, must be obeyed; and the seal of his teeth is a sure sign of the correctness of the orders. No mistake is possible.' He then commanded an outcaste wretch to pluck out his eyes. The order was obeyed, and the prince, accompanied by his faithful wife, wandered forth in sightless misery to beg his bread.

In the course of their weary wanderings they arrived at Pataliputra. 'Alas,' cried the blind man, 'what pain I suffer from cold and hunger. I was a prince; I am a beggar. Would that I could make myself known, and get redress for the false accusations brought against me!' He managed to penetrate into an inner court of the palace, where he lifted up his voice and wept, and, to the sound of a lute, sang a song full of sadness.

The king in an upper chamber heard the strains, and

thinking that he recognized the voice and touch as those of his son, sent for the minstrel. The king, when he beheld his sightless son, was overwhelmed with grief, and inquired by whose contrivance all this misery had come about. The prince humbly replied: 'In truth, for lack of filial piety I have thus been punished by Heaven. On such and such a day suddenly came a loving order, and I, having no means of excusing myself, dared not shrink from the punishment.'

The king, knowing in his heart that Queen Tishyarakshita was guilty of the crime, without further inquiry caused her to be burnt alive, and visited with condign punishment every person, high or low, who had any share in the outrage. The officials were some dismissed, some banished, some executed. The common people were, according to one account, massacred, and, according to another, transported across the Himalayas to the deserts of Khoten.

In those days a great saint named Ghosha dwelt in the monastery by the holy tree of Mahabodhi. To him the king brought Kunala, and prayed that his son might receive his sight. The saint commanded that on the morrow a great congregation should assemble to hear his preaching of the Law, and that each person should bring a vessel to receive his tears. A vast multitude of men and women assembled, and there was not one of those who heard the sermon but was moved to tears, which fell into the vessels provided.

The saint collected the tears in a golden vase, and said these words: 'The doctrine which I have expounded is the most mysterious of Buddha's teaching; if that exposition is not true, if there is error in what I have said, then let things remain as they are; but, if what I have said is true and free from error, let this man, after washing his eyes with these tears, receive his sight.'

Whereupon Kunala washed in the tears and received his

sight.

Tishyarakshita, queen of King Ashoka, in pursuance of her incestuous passion for her stepson, Prince Kunala, who repulsed her advances, resolved to avenge herself, and, in order to accomplish her purpose, took advantage of the king's sufferings from a dangerous and apparently incurable disease, to acquire complete control over his mind, and for some days she was granted unrestrained use of the sovereign power.

Ashoka, believing his malady to he incurable, gave the order: 'Send for Kunala; I wish to place him on the throne. What use is life to me?' Tishyarakshita hearing these words, thought to herself: 'If Kunala ascends the throne, I am lost.' Accordingly she said to King Ashoka: 'I undertake to restore you to health, but a necessary condition is that you forbid all physicians to have access to the palace.' The king complied with her request, and she enjoined everybody to bring to her any person, man or woman, who might be suffering from the same malady as the king.

Now it happened that a man of the shepherd caste was suffering from the same malady. His wife explained his case to a physician, who promised to prescribe a suitable remedy after examining the patient. The man then consulted the physician, who brought him to Queen Tishyarakshita. She had him conveyed to a secret place, where he was put to death. When his body was opened she perceived in his stomach a huge worm, which had deranged the bodily functions. She applied pounded pepper and ginger without effect, but when the worm was touched with an onion, he died immediately, and passed out of the intestines. The queen then begged the king to eat an onion and so recover his health. The king replied: 'Queen, I am a Kshatriya; how can I eat an onion?'

'My lord,' answered the queen, 'you should swallow it

merely as physic in order to save your life.' The king then ate the onion, and the worm died, passing out of the intestines.

The king resolved to give a thousand millions of gold pieces to the Master's service, and when far advanced in years had actually given nine hundred and sixty millions. In the hope that the vow would be completed before he died he daily sent great treasures of silver and gold to the Kukkutarama monastery at the capital. In those days Sampadi, the son of Kunala, was heir-apparent. To him the ministers pointed out that the king was ruining himself by his extravagance, and would, if permitted to continue it, be unable to resist the attacks of other monarchs or to protect the kingdom.

The prince, therefore, forbade the treasurer to comply with the king's demands. Ashoka, unable to obtain supplies from the treasury, began to give away the plate which furnished the royal table, first the gold, next the silver, and finally the iron. When all the metallic ware had been exhausted, the ministers furnished the king's table with earthenware. Then Ashoka demanded of them, 'Who is king of this country?' The ministers did obeisance and respectfully replied: 'Your majesty is king.' Ashoka burst into tears, and cried: 'Why do you say from kindness what is not true? I am fallen from my royal state. Save this half-apple there is nought of which I can dispose as sovereign.' Then the king sent the half-apple to the Kukkutarama monastery, to be divided among the monks, who should be addressed in this wise: 'Behold, this is my last gift; to this pass have come the riches of the emperor of India. My royalty and my power have departed; deprived of health, of physic, and of physicians, to me no support is left save that of the Assembly of the saints. Eat this fruit, which is offered with the intent that the whole Assembly may partake of it, my last gift.'

Once more King Ashoka asked his minister Radhagupta: 'Who is sovereign of this country?' The minister did obeisance and respectfully replied: 'Sire, your majesty is sovereign of this country.'

King Ashoka, recovering his composure, responded in verse, and said:

'This earth, encinctured by its sapphire zone,
This earth, bedecked with gleaming jewels rare,
 This earth, of hills the everlasting throne,
This earth, of all creation mother fair,
I give to the Assembly.
The blessing which attends such gift be mine;
Not Indra's halls nor Brahma's courts I crave,
Nor yet the splendours which round monarchs shine,
And pass away, like rushing Ganga's wave,
Abiding not a moment.
With faith unchangeable, which nought can shake,
This gift of Earth's immeasurable sphere
I to the Saints' Assembly freely make;
And self-control I crave, of boons most dear,
A good which changeth never.'

King Ashoka, having thus spoken, sealed the deed of gift, and presently fulfilled the law of mortality.

The forty millions of gold pieces which yet remained to complete King Ashoka's vow for the gift of a thousand millions, were expended by the ministers in the redemption of the earth, and Sampadi was placed upon the vacant throne. He was succeeded by his son Vrihaspati, who was succeeded in order by Vrishasena, Pushyadharma, and Pushpamitra.

The Edicts of Ashoka

The tendency for ancient rulers to have various types of messages inscribed in stone seems to have been pretty widespread. A great deal has been learned from inscriptions set up by the ancient Egyptians in particular although, as in the case of the Ashoka edicts, the key to a forgotten alphabet had to be found before the hieroglyphic messages of the Pharaohs of the Nile could tell modern people anything useful.

The impulse to record ideas, events, or something about the life of a person or people on some enduring material still survives today in the endless plaques unveiled by royalty, politicians and officials to mark, for instance, the opening of new buildings. Many modern statues also have explanatory inscriptions, and people still have details about their departed loved ones engraved on headstones. The aesthetic effect of the architecture of many churches, particularly in England, is frankly compromised by the presence of far too many stone and metal plaques bearing inscriptions commemorating the lives of dead parishioners and clergy.

Many ancient Roman inscriptions shamelessly glorify the lives and achievements of the individuals or families who caused them to be made. They often sit prominently on the side of a building or altar erected by the relevant individual, family or army legion. It might be argued that by giving details of the glittering career of some eminent senator, such inscriptions were pointing the way to virtue and accomplishment for any members of the next generation who might find themselves reading the inscription in future years, and indeed some ancient inscriptions and other texts are explicitly intended to do this; but an honest account of a life, with 'warts and all' might prove more useful for later generations struggling to work out how they are to live their own lives.

The first of the Ashoka edicts printed below is known to scholars as Ashoka's Major Rock Edict XIII. A plaque bearing a partial Greek version of this edict was discovered in Old Kandahar in Afghanistan in 1963. After looting in the 1990s, the whereabouts of this Greek version of part of Edict XIII is now unknown. The fact that the edict was placed in this Greek-speaking area in the local language is entirely consistent with the nature of Ashoka's own approach to his vast edict project. As he himself tells us in one of his own edicts:

This set of edicts of the Law of Piety has been written by command of His Majesty King Priyadarsin in a form sometimes condensed, sometimes of medium length, and sometimes expanded; for everything is not suitable in every place, and my dominions are extensive.

This flexibility was evidently also applied to the languages and alphabets in which Ashoka's edicts were inscribed.

Major Rock Edict XIII contrasts with many such inscriptions, both ancient and modern, because it does not merely glorify the ruler who had it made (detailing his victories in battle, for instance) but includes what seems to be a heart-felt confession from Ashoka about the ghastly errors of his early reign.

Here, his victory against the Kalingas is shown to be nothing to boast about, but is, on the contrary, a source of profound regret. The inscription bares the soul of its *onlie begetter*, which is most unusual.

Elsewhere in the edicts as presented by Vincent Smith we get insights into the limitations Ashoka placed on the degree to which his rule would be open and enlightened in the modern sense. There is little hint here, for instance, of anything resembling democracy: the emperor insists that his orders are absolute and final, and must be followed to the letter.

It seems that he regards himself as a father-figure, but not only of his own people: all men are his children, and he wants to promote their happiness. Whether all of his subjects, and others who found themselves within the sphere of Ashoka's influence, accepted him as their father is unclear.

In some of his edicts, Ashoka seems to be expressing a burning sense of responsibility for the happiness of others, as opposed to a mere desire to help them. Remarkably, he sees this responsibility as applicable not only to his own human subjects, but also to people living on and beyond his borders, and even to animals.

In his edicts Ashoka lays down amazingly modern rules about how animals should be treated. This is entirely consistent with Buddhist ideas of compassion, inspired in part by the idea that a living human might once have lived as an animal, and might be re-born as an animal in a later life.

Time and again in the edicts Ashoka states that his central concern is not with this present life, but with the afterlife. For him, it seems, present health, happiness and wisdom are most useful in that they bring his subjects to a better understanding of their place in the Buddhist universe, and offer them a chance to break the wheel of repeated re-birth.

The emperor's commitment to religious tolerance, as

expressed in the edicts, has been questioned on the grounds that in the India of the third century BCE Ashoka and his agents would not have come across any believers with ideas wildly divergent from their own. The Buddhism that he promulgated shared many ideas with the Hinduism out of which it had grown. Ashoka's insistence, in some of his edicts, that his subjects should seek to understand the core essentials of their own religions may reflect a belief that all the local sects shared a common core, and only differed in outward appearance and inessentials. Such ideas are still to be met with today among people who work to reconcile people of different faiths and sects.

Repeatedly, Ashoka insists on the importance of hard work – his own, and that of his officials and others – as the only way to bring about the inner and outer changes he wants to see. Impatience is expressed in parts of his edicts about his officials and their approach to their work: he also makes clear his determination to speed up the machinery of government, insisting that messages should be brought to him at all hours, wherever he happens to be, so that he can solve problems and make decisions promptly.

That Ashoka sited his remarkable edicts all over his vast empire and beyond gives us an impression of his piety and compassion; but the size and scope of what we might call his 'edict project' is also a demonstration of a level of personal power that might make modern, democratically-minded people a little uneasy. Immense effort evidently went into making these often very impressive and enduring artefacts, and not all of the effort would have been Ashoka's.

I have made few changes to Vincent Smith's version of the edicts I have selected for inclusion here. In particular, I have not substituted the important word *Dharma* for Smith's more familiar English equivalents. The ideas and language of Buddhism and other eastern religions are better known in the west in the twenty-first century than they were in Smith's time. Many westerners have embraced versions of Buddhism and Hinduism, and terms such as *Karma* and *Avatar*, for instance, both of which were originally Sanskrit words, are now well-known to many.

Lion capital of Ashoka at Sarnath, Uttar Pradesh.
Photo by Madho Prasad, c.1905

True Conquest

His Majesty King Priyadarsin in the ninth year of his reign conquered the Kalingas.

One hundred and fifty thousand persons were thence carried away captive, one hundred thousand were there slain, and many times that number perished.

Ever since the annexation of the Kalingas, His Majesty has zealously protected the Law of Piety, has been devoted to that law, and has proclaimed its precepts.

His Majesty feels remorse on account of the conquest of the Kalingas, because, during the subjugation of a previously unconquered country, slaughter, death, and taking away captive of the people necessarily occur, whereat His Majesty feels profound sorrow and regret.

There is, however, another reason for His Majesty feeling still more regret, inasmuch as in such a country dwell Brahmans and ascetics, men of different sects, and householders, who all practise obedience to elders, obedience to father and mother, obedience to teachers, proper treatment of friends, acquaintances, comrades, relatives, slaves and servants, with fidelity of devotion. To such people dwelling in that country happen violence, slaughter, and separation from those whom they love.

Even those persons who are themselves protected retain their affections undiminished: ruin falls on their friends, acquaintances, comrades, and relatives, and in this way violence is done to those who are personally unhurt. All this diffused misery is matter of regret to His Majesty. For there is no country where such communities are not found, including others besides Brahmans and ascetics, nor is there any place in any country where the people are not attached to some one sect or other.

The loss of even the hundredth or the thousandth part of the persons who were then slain, carried away captive, or done to death in Kalinga would now he a matter of deep regret to His Majesty.

Although a man should do him an injury, His Majesty holds that it must be patiently borne, so far as it can possibly be borne.

Even upon the forest tribes in his dominions His Majesty has compassion, and he seeks their conversion, inasmuch as the might even of His Majesty is based on repentance. They are warned to this effect: 'Shun evil-doing, that ye may escape destruction'; because His Majesty desires for all animate beings security, control over the passions, peace of mind, and joyousness.

And this is the chiefest conquest, in His Majesty's opinion: the conquest by the Law of Piety; this also is that effected by His Majesty both in his own dominions and in all the neighbouring realms as far as six hundred leagues, even to where the Greek king named Antiochus dwells, and beyond that Antiochus to where dwell the four kings severally named Ptolemy, Antigonus, Magas, and Alexander; and in the south, the kings of the Cholas, and Pandyas, and of Ceylon and likewise here, in the king's dominions, among the Yonas, and Kambojas, in Nabhaka of the Nabhitis, among the Bhojas and Pitinikas, among the Andhras and Pulindas, everywhere men follow the Law of Piety as proclaimed by His Majesty.

Even in those regions where the envoys of His Majesty

do not penetrate, men now practise and will continue to practise the Law of Piety as soon as they hear the pious proclamation of His Majesty issued in accordance with the Law of Piety.

And the conquest which has thereby been everywhere effected causes a feeling of delight.

Delight is found in the conquests made by the Law. Nevertheless, that delight is only a small matter. His Majesty thinks nothing of much importance save what concerns the next world.

And for this purpose has this pious edict been written, to wit, that my sons and grandsons, as many as they may be, may not suppose it to be their duty to effect a new conquest; and that even when engaged in conquest by arms they may find pleasure in patience and gentleness, and may regard as the only true conquest that which is effected through the Law of Piety, which avails both for this world and the next. Let all their pleasure be the pleasure in exertion, which avails both for this world and the next.

The Practice of Piety

For a long time past, even for many hundred years, the slaughter of living creatures, cruelty to animate beings, disrespect to relatives, and disrespect to Brahmans and ascetics, have grown. But now, by reason of the practice of piety by His Majesty King Priyadarsin, instead of the sound of the war-drum, the sound of the drum of piety is heard, while heavenly spectacles of processional cars, elephants, illuminations, and the like, are displayed to the people by His Majesty, the sound of the war-drum, or rather the sound of the law of piety is heard, bringing with it the display of heavenly spectacles.

As for many hundred years past has not happened, at this present, by reason of His Majesty King Priyadarsin's proclamation of the law of piety, the cessation of slaughter of living creatures, the prevention of cruelty to animate beings, respect to relatives, respect to Brahmans and ascetics, obedience to parents and obedience to elders, are growing. Thus, and in many other ways, the practice of piety is growing, and His Majesty King Priyadarsin will cause that practice to grow still more.

The sons, grandsons, and great-grandsons of His Majesty King Priyadarsin will promote the growth of that practice until the end of the cycle, and, abiding in piety and morality, will proclaim the law of piety; for the best of all deeds is the proclamation of the law of piety, and the practice of piety is not for the immoral man. In this matter growth is good, and not to decrease is good. For this very purpose has this writing been made, in order that men may in this matter strive for growth, and not suffer decrease. This has been written by command of His Majesty King Priyadarsin in the thirteenth year of his reign.

The Prompt Dispatch of Business

Thus saith his Majesty King Priyadarsin: For a long time past business has not been disposed of, nor have reports been received at all hours. I have accordingly arranged that at all hours and in all places, whether I am dining or in the ladies' apartments, in my bedroom, or in my closet, in my carriage, or in the palace gardens, the official reporters should keep me constantly informed of the people's business, which business of the people I am ready to dispose of at any place.

And if, perchance, I personally by word of mouth command that a gift be made or an order executed, or anything urgent is entrusted to the officials, and in that business a dispute arises or fraud occurs among the clergy, I have commanded that immediate report must be made to me at any hour and at any place, for I am never fully satisfied with my exertions and my dispatch of business.

Work I must for the public benefit, and the root of the matter is in exertion and dispatch of business, than which nothing is more efficacious for the general welfare. And for what do I toil? For no other end than this, that I may discharge my debt to animate beings, and that while I make some happy in this world, they may in the next world gain heaven. For this purpose have I caused this pious edict to be written, that it may long endure, and that my sons, grandsons, and great-grandsons may strive for the public weal; though that is a difficult thing to attain, save by the utmost toil.

Pious Tours

In times past Their Majesties used to go out on so-called tours of pleasure, during which hunting and other similar amusements used to be practised. His Majesty King Priyadarsin, however, in the eleventh year of his reign, went out on the road leading to true knowledge, whence originated tours devoted to piety, during which are practised the beholding of ascetics and Brahmans, with liberality to them, the beholding of elders, largess of gold, the beholding of the country and the people, proclamation of the law of piety, and discussion of the law of piety.

Consequently, since that time, these are the pleasures of His Majesty King Priyadarsin, in exchange for those of the past.

True Glory

His Majesty King Priyadarsin does not believe that glory and renown bring much profit unless the people both in the present and the future obediently hearken to the Law of Piety, and conform to its precepts.

For that purpose only does His Majesty King Priyadarsin desire glory and renown. But whatsoever exertions His Majesty King Priyadarsin has made, all are for the sake of the life hereafter, so that every one may be freed from peril, which peril is sin. Difficult, verily, it is to attain such freedom, whether people be of low or of high degree, save by the utmost exertion and complete renunciation; but this is for those of high degree extraordinarily difficult.

True Charity

There is no such charity as the charitable gift of the Law of Piety, no such friendship as the friendship in piety, no such distribution as the distribution of piety, no such kinship as kinship in piety. The Law of Piety consists in these things, to wit, kind treatment of slaves and servants, obedience to father and mother, charity to ascetics and Brahmans, respect for the sanctity of life. Therefore a father, son, brother, master, friend, or comrade, nay even a neighbour, ought to say: 'This is meritorious, this ought to be done.' He who acts thus both gains this world and begets infinite merit in the next world, by means of this very charity of the Law of Piety.

Toleration

His Majesty King Priyadarsin does reverence to men of all sects, whether ascetics or householders, by donations and various modes of reverence. His Majesty, however, cares not so much for donations or external reverence as that there should be a growth of the essence of the matter in all sects. The growth of the essence of the matter assumes various forms, but the root of it is restraint of speech, to wit, a man must not do reverence to his own sect by disparaging that of another man for trivial reasons.

Depreciation should be for adequate reasons only, because the sects of other people deserve reverence for one reason or another. By thus acting, a man exalts his own sect, and at the same time does service to the sects of other people. By acting contrariwise, a man hurts his own sect, and does disservice to the sects of other people. For he who does reverence to his own sect, while disparaging all other sects from a feeling of attachment to his own, on the supposition that he thus glorifies his own sect, in reality by such conduct inflicts severe injury on his own sect.

Self-control, therefore, is meritorious, to wit, hearkening to the law of others, and hearkening willingly, and that such communication is better than any material almsgiving.

For this is His Majesty's desire, that adherents of all sects should be fully instructed and sound in doctrine. The adherents of the several sects must be informed that His

Majesty cares not so much for donations or external reverence as that there should be a growth, and a large growth, of the essence of the matter in all sects.

The Borderers' Edict

Thus saith His Majesty: At Samapa the officials are to be instructed in the king's commands as follows: I desire my views to be practically acted upon and carried into effect by suitable means; and, in my opinion, the principal means for accomplishing this object are my instructions to you. All men are my children, and, just as for my children I desire that they should enjoy all happiness and prosperity both in this world and in the next, so for all men I desire the like happiness and prosperity. If you ask what is the king's will concerning the border tribes, I reply that my will is this concerning the borderers; that they should be convinced that the King desires them to be free from disquietude.

I desire them to trust me and to be assured that they will receive from me happiness, not sorrow, and to be convinced that the King bears them good will, and I desire that (whether to win my good will or merely to please me) they should practise the Law of Piety, and so gain both this world and the next. And for this purpose I give you instructions.

When in this manner I have once for all given you my instructions and signified my orders, then my resolutions and my promises are immutable. Understanding this, do your duty, and inspire these folk with trust, so that they may be convinced that the King is unto them even as a father, and that, as he cares for himself, so he cares for them, who are as the king's children. Having given you my instructions, and notified to you my orders, my resolutions and promises being immutable, I expect to be well served by you in this business, because you are in a position enabling you to inspire these folk with trust and to secure their happiness and prosperity both in this world and in the next; and by so acting you will gain heaven and discharge your debt to me.

It is for this purpose that this edict has been inscribed here in order that the officials may display persevering energy in inspiring trust in these borderers and guiding them in the path of piety. This edict should be recited every four months at the Tishya Nakshatra festival, and at discretion, as occasion offers, in the intervals, it should be recited to individuals. Take care by acting thus to direct people in the right way.

The Duties of Officials
to the Provincials

By command of His Majesty: At Tosali the officers in charge of the administration of the city are to be instructed as follows: I desire my views to be practically acted upon and carried into effect by suitable means; and, in my opinion, the principal means for accomplishing this object are my instructions to you; for you have been set over many thousands of living beings to gain the affection of good men.

All men are my children, and, just as for my children I desire that they should enjoy all happiness and prosperity both in this world and in the next, so for all men I desire the like happiness and prosperity. You, however, do not gain the best possible results. There are individuals who heed only part of my teaching and not the whole. You must see to such persons so that the moral rule may be observed. There are, again, individuals who have been put in prison or to torture. You must be at hand to stop unwarranted imprisonment or torture. Again, many there are who suffer acts of violence. It should be your desire to set such people in the right way.

There are, however, certain dispositions which render success impossible; namely, envy, lack of perseverance, harshness, impatience, want of application, idleness, indolence. You, therefore, should desire to be free from such dispositions, inasmuch as the root of all this teaching consists in perseverance and patience in moral guidance.

He who is indolent does not rise to his duty, and yet an officer should bestir himself, move forward, go on. The same holds good for your duty of supervision. For this reason I must repeat to you, 'Consider and know that such and such are His Majesty's instructions.'

Fulfilment of these orders bears great fruit, non-fulfilment brings great calamity. By officers who fail to give such guidance neither the favour of heaven nor the favour of the King is to be hoped for. My special insistence on this duty is profitable in two ways, for by following this line of conduct you will both win heaven and discharge your debt to me. This edict must be recited at every Tishya Nakshatra festival, and at intervals between Tishyas, as occasion offers, it should be read to individuals. And do you take care by acting thus to direct people in the right way.

For this purpose has this edict been inscribed here in order that the officers in charge of the city may display persevering zeal to prevent unwarranted imprisonment or unwarranted torture of the citizens. And for this purpose, in accordance with the Law of Piety, every five years I shall cause to be summoned to the Assembly those men who are mild, patient, and who respect life, in order that hearing these things they may act according to my instructions.

And the Prince of Ujjain shall for the same purpose summon an Assembly of the same kind, but he must perform this duty every three years without fail. The same order applies to Taxila. The officials attending the Assembly, while not neglecting their special duties, will also learn this teaching, and must see that they act according to the king's instructions.

The Royal Example

Thus saith His Majesty King Piyadasi: The Law of Piety is excellent. But what is the Law of Piety? It requires innocuousness, many good deeds, compassion, truthfulness, purity. The gift of spiritual insight I have given in manifold ways; whilst on two-footed and four-footed beings, on birds, and on the denizens of the waters I have conferred many benefactions even unto the boon of life; and many other good deeds have I done.

For this purpose I have caused this pious edict to be written, that men may walk after its teaching, and that it may long endure; and he who will follow its teaching will do well.

Self-Examination

Thus saith His Majesty King Piyadasi: Man sees his every good deed, and says, 'This good deed have I done.' In no wise does he see his evil deed and say, 'This evil deed, this thing in the nature of sin, have I done.'

Difficult, verily, is the needful self-examination. Nevertheless, a man should see to this; that rage, cruelty, anger, pride, and jealousy are in the nature of sin, and should say, 'Let me not by reason of these things bring about my fall. This is chiefly to be seen to. The one course avails me for the present world, the other course avails me at any rate for the world to come.'

Select Bibliography

Allen, Charles: *Ashoka*, Abacus, 2013

Campbell, Joseph: *The Hero With A Thousand Faces*, New World Library, 2012

Gethin, Robert: *The Foundations of Buddhism*, Opus, 1998

Kerouac, Jack; *The Dharma Bums*, Penguin, 2011

Lodge, David (ed.): *20th Century Literary Criticism*, Longman, 1972

Nehru, Jawaharlal: *India's Quest*, Asia Publishing House, 1963

Smith, Vincent A: *Asoka*, Oxford, 1901

Smith, Vincent A.: *Indian Constitutional Reform Viewed by the Light of History*, Oxford, 1919

Strong, John S.: *The Legend of King Asoka*, Princeton, 1989

Wallis Budge, E.A.: *Egyptian Tales and Romances*, Thornton Butterworth, 1935

Wells, H.G.: *Outline of History*, Garden City, 1920

Note on the Text

Because an e-book version of this title is in preparation, I have decided to spell Sanskrit and other Indian words and names without the diacritical marks which are often seen: much modern e-reader software still cannot cope with these. The different authors from whom the extracts above are taken spell the name 'Ashoka' differently in their original texts: I have changed these to 'Ashoka' throughout.

Glossary

asoka tree: a rain-forest tree found in India: *Saraca asoca.*

Ashokarama: a Buddhist monastery Ashoka had built in Patalipura, the modern Indian city of Patna.

bo tree: a type of fig tree sacred to Buddhists because Gautama is said to have attained enlightenment while sitting under such a tree.

Brahmins/ Brahmans: in this context, Hindu religious leaders.

chaitya: in India, a prayer-hall or other sacred space.

deva: in Buddhism, a higher being.

eightfold path: 'right view, right resolve, right speech, right conduct, right livelihood, right effort, right mindfulness, and right union. Buddhist art often features designs with eight parts or points. In the legends of Ashoka the remains of the Buddha are said to have been housed in eight stupas, and the cutting from the bo-tree planted in Sri Lanka gives off eight shoots.

Gautama: name for the Buddha.

Jina: 'the victorious one': another name for the Buddha.

Kathavatthu: a treatise dealing with various controversial issues within Buddhism, supposedly written in Ashoka's time.

Kshatriya: the ruling and military class in traditional Hindu society.

Lakh: one hundred thousand.

Magadha: ancient Indian kingdom in the south of Bihar.

marks of sanctity: there are said to be 112 physical signs that a man might be a Buddha, or a great man, of which 32 are primary signs. These include long, slender fingers, smooth, golden skin, forty teeth and a long, broad tongue.
outcaste: in traditional Hindu societies, a person with no caste – such a person might have been excluded from their caste.
Porus or **Poros**: Indian king said to have been defeated by Alexander the great, who then set him up as a 'satrap' (see below)
Ptolemies: Egyptian rulers of Greek extraction; from the name of Ptolemy I Soter, founder of the dynasty.
Sakyas: clan or ethnic group into which Gautama was born.
satrap: governor or surrogate, subsidiary leader, in this context in the Hellenistic world.
Seleucids: ruling Hellenistic dynasty, founded by Seleucus I Nicator.
seven steps: the Buddha is supposed to have walked seven steps an instant after having been born.
Sthavira: early sect or school of Buddhism
Taxila: ancient area of India. The ruins of Taxila City can now be seen in the Punjab.
tirthyas: non-Buddhist teachers.
Vaibadhyavadina: ancient Buddhist sect.

For free downloads and more from the Langley Press, please visit our website at:

http://tinyurl.com/lpdirect

25408772R00047

Printed in Great Britain
by Amazon